GW00818822

Advent preparing for Christ

Hope, Peace, Joy and Love

By Rev. Canon Jim Shoucair and Richard Mathews

Forward:

It is the best of times.

It is the worst of times.

Yet should not Advent always be a time the world turns aside from our daily trials and tribulation?

Should not Advent be a time to remember the reason for the season celebrating the greatest present of all, Jesus?

The following collection of Advent reflections and seasonal thoughts represent my humble attempt to put the often hectic Holiday Season into perspective.

Yet, if you believe I am not as guilty as any of forgetting the true reason for the season during Advent, you are incorrect my friends.

As the father of four, shopping for presents, decorating for Christmas, and all the other additional activities which today often dominate the Advent season more than once turned me into a symbolic Scrooge.

Fortunately like Charles Dicken's Scrooge , I have slowly begun to realize, the most important present of the Advent season is the time spent with those we love whether in worship or with family and friends in celebration.

May the words I have written help you draw closer to the true reason for the season the greatest gift of all, the present of Jesus.

The First Sunday of Advent

"Be Watchful Be Alert"

Gospel: Mark 13: 33-37

Jesus said to his disciples:

"Be watchful! Be alert!

You do not know when the time will come.

It is like a man traveling abroad.

He leaves home and places his servants in charge, each with his own work, and orders the gatekeeper to be on the watch.

Watch, therefore; you do not know when the Lord of the house is coming, whether in the evening, or at midnight, or at cockcrow, or in the morning. May he not come suddenly and find you sleeping.

What I say to you, I say to all: 'Watch!'"

The world's journey through Advent in preparation for the celebration of the birth of Jesus on Christmas begins on Sunday.

Yet whether any follow the Christian faith or not, the secular messages of Advent are lessons in life worthy of your consideration.

Many remain dismayed at my contention the love you share with family and friends is of greater worth to your emotional, physical and yes spiritual condition than materialistic assets.

I hope and pray even those who value their wealth over the love of others can agree, the life lessons of Advent hold significant value to mankind.

The first week of Advent traditionally asks us to consider, three uniquely human liabilities;

1)   Our human frailties be they physical, emotional or even financial in nature,

2)   Our human response to the same which limits our ability to achieve our potential,

3)   Our human disposition regarding preparation to receive the bounty of the greatest gift of all.

Leaving the spiritual call of Advent to return to the secular world of many, let me ask you how many times you have fallen into adversity because;

1)   You overestimated your own assets whatever they may be

2)   You did not accept the assistance or advice of others to achieve a goal

3)   You deemed a possibility ended and never followed through open to future achievement.

While I hope none of the prior actions have ever occurred in your life, I have had all three such situations represent exactly why I allowed opportunity to slip from my grasp with none to actually blame but myself!

It is from this hard fact learned in my life I came to believe the life lessons of Advent hold value for all to consider.

Let us continue to explore how the traditional spiritual messages of Advent can be applied to the secular world. Let us explore the opportunity for all to enhance our communal understanding of our fellow man in our journey through life.

Let us consider the words of Pope Francis,

"Open your hearts to accept all people radiating the peace of the Lord living always to love one another, Amen."

Reflections during 1st Week of Advent

"React Radiating Peace"

Few ever harnessed the power of peace more gracefully than Dr. Martin Luther King, Jr.

In this time of growing civil unrest, let us take a moment to consider the power of reacting by radiating peace.

We all know someone who no matter the volatility of the situation can instantly restore calm.

The type of person whose very presence changes chaos to order.

The individual who develops compromise and closure in even the most difficult of situations.

Today we look at those who react by radiating peace.

When we were children, often one parent or family member filled the role of peace maker.

As we grew many met a teacher or coach who held that special personality trait which stabilized any situation.

During our work careers, most of us have had a supervisor or even a co-worker whom all turned to in time of trouble for their peace making skills.

While some accomplish this feat owing to their stature or authority in society, others establish peace by radiating the same in their reactions to life.

Yet, the informal peace makers come in all shapes and sizes. They are young and young at heart. They are blessed with wisdom or sometimes simply blessed with a caring heart.

No matter their age, shape or level of education, they reject the anger, outrage or discord of the world itself.

John 16:33 *"I have told you these things, so that in me you may have peace. In this world you will have trouble. But take heart! I have overcome the world."*

The Peace makers react to life through the lens of peace. Peace which holds no value in the emphasis of our common errors. Peace which sees no value in blame or scorn. Peace which knows overcoming our troubles requires forgiveness and closure.

The next time you find yourself tempted to fuel the fire of rage or even simply continue a blaze of passion ignited by emotion, attempt instead to react radiating peace.

You just might find that in time, you too will be known as a Peace maker.

Matthew 5:9 *"Blessed are the **peace** makers, for they will be called children of God."*

"Peace on Earth, Goodwill to Men."

Peace on Earth has rarely been a more universal goal than today.

Yet for millions the concept of achieving Peace on Earth appears only a remote possibility reflective of the Terrorist actions which have occurred and Civil War confronting millions across the globe.

For millions more the concept of finding Peace in our far too hectic days simply preparing for Christmas remains a challenge.

But to you my friends, I pray my humble thoughts over the coming days will grant you some level of Peace.

Peace gained in prayer reflecting on what is truly the greatest present of all God's love manifested in our Lord and Savior Jesus Christ.

Let us reflect on the miracle of Jesus.

A miracle which fulfilled a thousand years of Old Testament prophecy.

A miracle which began God's plan to truly bring Peace on Earth.

Let us remember the words of Luke 2:14, *"Glory to God in the Highest, and Peace on Earth to all whom God is pleased."*

"God is our refuge and our Strength."

Energy or in my case, lack of same, is one of the things in life I continue to blame time for stealing.

Is it only me or did any of you used to have more energy?

Conversely, as time marches on, could it be we allow perceived obligations to drain our batteries as I have done more than once leaving the lights on in my car?

Far too often during the Holidays, I find myself attempting to do too many things which truly do not bring me any closer to God.

I find myself consumed in activities which do not allow me to share the love of the Christmas season with family and friends.

At these times I need to turn to God in Prayer for guidance in sorting out my priorities.

So the next time you feel like you just can't find the time or the energy to handle the hectic and hurry of the Christmas season consider turning to the Lord in prayer.

Let us remember the words of Psalm 46.1, *"God is our refuge and strength, an ever present help in our trouble."*

*"**Be devoted to one another in brotherly love.**"*

Attitude check time has arrived.

All too soon Christmas Day will be here.

Are the Christmas cards ready?

Have you found that special gift for your most special someone?

Have you finished decorating the house?

Then again, if any or all of the above didn't happen, would that actually stop your celebration of Christmas?

There were times the house really did not get decorated.

There were times we couldn't send many Christmas cards.

There were times what few Christmas presents we could buy were extremely limited.

But looking back at those days, they were filled with the greatest present of all, love.

Love shared simply yet in true Christian fellowship with family and friends.

Let us remember the words of Romans 12: 10, *"Be devoted to one another in brotherly love; give preference to one another in honor"*

The second Sunday of Advent, "Peace."

Perhaps the time has come for the secular world to consider the value of Christian hope for Peace.

In my journey through life, few worldly troubles concern me more deeply than the growing loss of hope by particularly today's Millennials, my children's generation.

Millennials are not following the traditional paths of faith their parents or grandparents chose.

Multiple reasons have been put forth by both Religious and Secular Scholars for the decline in religious participation particularly in Europe and the United States.

Many secular scholars contend that,

"As mankind has become increasing confident in his ability to understand his world, spirituality in all forms represents an intellectual conflict."

Conversely religious scholars portray the central theme in declining Western based faiths to be related to,

"The church has not effectively addressed the evolution of man's spiritual needs."

I am neither a secular or theological scholar and will not pretend to know which answer is correct if either actually are.

What I do know if why I practice the Christian faith.

I am a Christian because I know I don't know all the answers to the mystery of life.

I am a Christian because I know I cannot change the world or even often the difficulties facing me professionally or personally without my fellow man empowered by God's grace.

I am a Christian because without, "Hope," I would never have summoned the strength to overcome hardships beyond my ability to contend with.

The word "hope" has two meanings in the Bible.

1) *Tiqvah*, contains the sense of eager anticipation or waiting.

2) E*lpis*. depicts a sense of confident expectation based on certainty.

Biblical hope is secured by God's faithfulness to His promises. For the Old Testament leaders, their hope was in the Messiah's arrival. For us, it is the hope of the Messiah's return.

The key point of today's reflection for both my Christian and secular friends to consider is,

"What form of hope should we be focusing on this week of Advent?"

Should be awaiting the return of the Messiah?

Should we be focused on the role we can fulfil in bringing Peace to Earth and Sharing Goodwill toward Man by loving our neighbors as ourselves?

Again, I do not know the correct answer.

What I do know is, "Hope for Peace," gives me the strength to often make the best of an admittedly poor situation.

"Peace," which can and does allow me to bring some joy and comfort to those whose lives I touch.

"Peace," viewed in the eyes of a child inspires me to turn wishes into reality.

I close with a question, *"Will you help bring peace to your world one day, one person, one instance at a time this week?"*

Reflections for the Second Week of Advent

"Be compassionate and humble."

Compassion is at least in my opinion, a Christian challenge we all fail to at times observe during the trials and tribulations which confront us.

Let us be honest, "Has anyone else found themselves unhappy or even actually being quite upset while stuck in Christmas season traffic?"

Perhaps once in your life have you found yourself wondering about the intelligence of the checkout clerk at the local mall?

Is it just me or does anyone else find the media noise of advertising simply infuriating at times?

Now comes the hard question, why?

Why do we allow ourselves to get upset about any of the above?

I know requesting you extend true love being compassionate to particularly strangers is asking a lot.

But I am going to ask anyway.

Let us remember the words of 1 Peter 3:8, *"Finally, all of you, be like-minded, be sympathetic, love one another, be compassionate and humble."*

"Finally, brothers, rejoice!"

Elation is defined as great happiness and exhilaration.

But to me, Elation's synonyms: euphoria, ecstasy, exultation and bliss are all equally appropriate words to describe the Christmas Feelings of Children.

The years have now past quickly since the days leading up to Christmas generating ever increasing elation by my children.

Yet the memories remain of the bliss which eventually settled in come Christmas Day.

Whether young or young at heart, today I ask you to consider unbridling your elation and sharing it with all you meet.

I contend, there is no greater reason for great happiness and exhilaration than our celebration of the birth of Jesus.

Today let us remember the words of 2 Corinthians 13:11, *"Finally, brothers, rejoice. Aim for restoration, comfort one another, agree with one another, live in peace; and the God of love and peace will be with you."*

Omnipotent, *"God working in you."*

Okay, Omnipotent isn't a word many of us use in common speech.

But we are discussing how to battle through the trials and tribulations leading up to Christmas day, right?

I will not attempt to wax poetic or worse prove my lack of theological education relating to God's power to accomplish the impossible to the improbable.

What I will note is, "God has always provided when I turned to him even if at times that provision was not the bounty I had hoped for or expected."

A few weeks ago I was feeling depressed about the events of the world. That mood quickly changed as I came upon a co-worker seemingly transfixed in a state of bliss.

I asked him what he was smiling about he noted. "I talked to my wife and we decided to give part of my Holiday bonus away."

When I asked him what he had done with his bonus he replied, "We went to Walmart and saw the manager. He helped us spread a little Christmas cheer paying off lay-away purchases."

God is Omnipotent my friends. But that does not mean we cannot do his will as his Angels on Earth.

How can you be an Angel for God today?

Let us remember the words of Philippines 2:13, *"For God is working in you, giving you the desire and power to do what pleases him."*

The third Candle of Advent is for, "Joy."

The 3rd week of Advent begins on Sunday with the lighting of the Pink candle, the candle of Joy.

Poet's note, "Hot pink, pale pink, rose pink are all shades of pink painted into a sunrise."

The shades of pink in nature are as diverse as the joys we respond to in life.

I do not know how you and those in your journey through life chose to express joy.

What I do know is, allowing my blinders on life to be removed opens my heart to experience joy in a wide array of opportunities.

Joy can be found in actions and activities far too diverse to note in this humble essay.

Joy can be found in a child's eyes, a friend's smile, a lover's touch a parent or grandparents embrace.

Paul tells us in 1 Thessalonians 5:16, **"To be joyful always!"**

Today I ask you, "Will you consider taking on the liability of becoming truly joyful?"

Allowing love, hope and joy into our lives does come with a cost. That cost is the realization; God blesses his world and his children.

Each night this week we should attempt to pause in gratitude.

Whatever the day has brought, no matter how busy it has been, we can stop, before we fall asleep, to give thanks for a little more light, a little more freedom to walk by that light, in joy.

Will you pay the price to bring the light of Joy into your life and the World?

Reflections for the Third Week of Advent

"No, is at times the answer of faith."

You might find considering the power of no an odd thought to help carry us through the Christmas season.

But at times, no can be the key to the greatest gifts of all as it opens up a world of even greater possibilities.

Four times my heart has been laid bare discussing Santa Claus with my children as they reached that age of questioning.

Four times I had to admit there was no Earthly Santa Claus.

Over that decade I came to realize, the spirit of selfless giving represented in Santa Claus is a miracle which I believe God must have inspired.

The celebration of Christmas has survived the now long forgotten rule of earthly Kings.

The celebration of Christmas has survived the hardship of natural disasters.

The celebration of Christmas has survived the tragedy of world wars.

May we never lose faith in the promise of love no matter how many times no stands in our way.

Let us remember the words of Hebrews 10:23, *"Let us hold unswervingly to the hope we profess, for he who promised to always love us remains eternally faithful."*

"Love Everyone!"

Well that my friends is a major challenge.

Is it even practical to attempt to show the Christmas spirit of giving and kindness to everyone?

In today's troubled times, is it even safe to encourage anyone to practice the great commandment to love they neighbor?

I really can't defend either action

But I refuse to live my life in fear.

Perhaps I have simply come to that point in life that I really don't care what the world thinks of my commitment to attempt to Live to Love each and every day.

Maybe just maybe four young men from Liverpool came to the same decision half a century ago professing in song,

"What the World Needs Now, Is Love Sweet Love. It's the Only Thing That There Is Just too Little Of."

My challenge to you today is, "Will you try to share the love of Jesus Christ with everyone this Christmas season?"

Let us remember the words of Matthew 22: 38-40,

"And Jesus said to him, "'YOU SHALL LOVE THE LORD YOUR GOD WITH ALL YOUR HEART, AND WITH ALL YOUR SOUL, AND WITH ALL YOUR MIND.'

"This is the great and foremost commandment. "The second is like it, 'YOU SHALL LOVE YOUR NEIGHBOR AS YOURSELF.'"

"Make Anytime Happen"

I keep searching for when anytime will arrive.

What I have learned is, resolving my anytime challenge requires a major commitment on my part.

Do you ever find yourself justifying putting things off with the contention, I can do that anytime?

During these last few days before Christmas, I challenge you to turn anytime into sometime very soon.

We should never worry about a friend saying, "Sorry I'm too busy to have lunch with you during the holiday season?"

We should never worry about a family member honesty telling us, "I can't come to your Holiday Party."

We should never worry about our spouse noting, "No, I just don't have time right now."

What we must though attempt to resolve is our very human nature to put off to tomorrow or anytime sharing the love and blessings of our family and friends.

Let us remember the words of. 2 Timothy 2:22, *"Instead, pursue righteous living, faithfulness,*

love, and peace. Enjoy the companionship of those
who call on the Lord with pure hearts."

The fourth candle of Advent,

"Love."

It is the irony of the Christian faith which most often brings me pause in my walk through the secular world.

I ask you all, does the 4th Sunday of Advent ever arrive to not find mankind desperately searching for the blessing of Peace?

Responsorial Psalm *Ps 24:5-6*

Let the Lord enter; he is king of glory.

He shall receive a blessing from the LORD,
a reward from God his savior.
Such is the race that seeks for him,
that seeks the face of the God of Jacob.

Let the Lord enter; he is king of glory.

The fourth candle reminds us that Jesus comes to bring Peace through love to both the world and to people's hearts.

In the lighting of the fourth candle, we have come full circle within the circle of life represented by the Advent Wreath.

We began our journey week one in watchfulness.

We carried on to our week two message of being filled with hope.

We faced the challenge of melding watchfulness and hope into a daily message of joy.

We now are charged with taking all we have learned wrapped with the peace manifested in the love of Christ this Christmas.

Is there a more important gift you can give anyone than your caring, hopeful, joyous life dedicated to sharing the peace and love of the Lord?

Until the end of times, there will be trials and tribulations between even the most loving of persons.

Until the end of times, there will be conflicts beyond the scope most if not all of us can attempt to resolve.

Until the end of times, there will be death, sickness and despair none of us will ever gain the ability to understand why it is occurring.

What we cannot allow all of the above to do is distract us from our potential to carry forth the Peace of Jesus Christ into our world.

Entering this fourth week of Advent I ask you to, "Give Peace a Chance!"

Reflection for the 4th Week of Advent

"Right, what is Morally Justified"

Right is in my opinion often forgotten to be additionally defined as morally justified. In my life, the decisions I've made which were morally justified were the most important.

As a manager in training for a national buffet chain restaurant, I had been taught from day one, "customers cannot take home food."

Yet for weeks I had watched every Tuesday as a young teenager brought her three younger siblings to the restaurant. When fortunate they would arrive just before Five O'clock able to take advantage of our lower lunch pricing.

Rotating through every staff position, I had even waited on these four young children who ordered no beverage, behaved wonderfully and had rarely taken more food than they could eat.

But one day, only three of the children arrived. Their waitress let me know, they were putting food in their pockets wrapped in napkins.

I had to do the right thing, right?

Fortunately I said a prayer for guidance as I walked to their table to find out what was going on. God provided.

I found out one sibling was too ill to come to dinner. The children admitted they were taking home food for their sister.

So I did the wrong thing.

I paid for another buffet. The waitress and staff helped me pack up a meal for the children to take home to their sibling. When we brought the meal to the children, our reward of smiles was priceless.

Today, will you try to do what is not just right by secular standards, will you try to do what is morally justified by God?

Let us remember the words of Colossians 3:17, *"And whatever you do, in word or deed, do everything in the name of the Lord Jesus, giving thanks to God the Father through him."*

"Trust a Modern Rarity a Pillar of Faith"

Trust is defined as our confident hope for that which is yet to occur.

Yet many contend Trust is fading in our complex, hurried world of often short term relationships.

Today, I ask you to consider that Trust might indeed be the most under-appreciated pillar of global society.

Does anyone truly doubt the lights in your home will work when you flip the switch?

Does anyone truly doubt water will come out of the faucet when you turn the handle?

Does anyone truly doubt there will be food at the grocery store or goods for purchase when you need to go shopping?

Even our very currency of exchange is built on Trust. We accept a piece of paper has value or more amazingly yet, a piece of plastic will compensate someone for the goods or services we purchase.

Today I ask you to extend your Trust beyond even our societal pillars of civilization.

Trust that God's peace is offered to you granting you his comfort and his bounty.

Let us remember the words of Romans 15:13, *"May the God of hope fill you with all joy and peace in believing, so that by the power of the Holy Spirit you may abound in hope."*

"Where there is Hope, Miracles Occur."

Hope next to love is perhaps the most powerful force in mans' history.

Hope helped carry the Jewish people throughout the Old Testament.

Hope kept the flame of freedom alive for peoples across the globe.

Hope today challenges all to reflect on the potential of ending Global Inequality which manifests itself in many forms from poverty to social and even religious intolerance.

My wife is famous for saying, "Can't we all get along."

Hers is a world view worthy of closing this series upon.

As we prepare to celebrate the Birth of Jesus on this Christmas Eve, let us reflect on hope.

Hope that joy shall soon fill all hearts.

Hope that peace on Earth shall come.

Hope that love will win the day.

Let us remember the words of Luke 2:11, ***"For unto you is born this day in the city of David a Savior, who is Christ the Lord."***

The fifth candle of Advent,

"The Christ Candle."

Whether among the very young or young at heart, the celebration of Christmas Day surpasses any other that occurs on an annual bases.

Across the globe Christmas unites billions in a day of sharing peace and joy. A day when the Christ Candle's light shines forth in love.

With the lighting of the fifth candle of Advent, the Christ Candle, the light of love is brought forth symbolically in exclamation of Jesus the Christ's birth on Earth.

Yet for many of the intellectually biased throughout the secular world, Christmas is not intended to celebrate the unrequested love of Jesus' birth. It is about the exchange of material possessions often purchased for reasons unbefitting the reason for the season.

I will not lie to you and contend I do not enjoy the creature comforts of modern life.

But I will contend that like many of you, my fondest treasures from Christmas past are forged in the memories created with the people I spent those wonderful holiday times.

The lighting of the Christ Candle this year while it will bring to a close this Advent series.

I pray our time united in thought will not be forgotten.

You my friends are bringing Christ's love, his light to our world.

From Taiwan to Argentina from the Philippians to the Ukraine from China to the United States, you have shared our journey through Advent.

You are bringing the Good News of Jesus the Christ to the world.

A world in need of caring, hopeful, joyous, peaceful people committed to loving their neighbors as they wish to be loved themselves.

No greater gift carries a deeper value for enhancing the common good than the Love represented in the Christ Candle of Advent.

The greatest gift of all at Christmas is ours.

"The Son of God was sent to save us all through love."

Merry Christmas to all.

Jesus Christ was born today.

Christmas has come and gone for many.

But for those who have never read about the symbolism in the 12 Days of Christmas, please reflect on the following.

Many have heard the song, the 12 Days of Christmas. But did you know;

The partridge in a pear tree represents the love and promise of peace in the birth of Jesus.

The two turtle doves are God's word to us given in the Old and New Testaments.

The three French hens symbolize, Faith, Hope and Love.

The four calling birds refer to the four Gospels of Matthew, Mark, Luke & John.

The five golden rings honor the Torah of Law the first five books of the Old Testament.

The six geese-a-laying stand for the six days in which God Created our World.

The seven swans-a-swimming expose the gifts of the Holy Spirit as Prophesy, Service, Teaching, Exhortation, Giving, Leadership and Compassion.

The eight maids-a-milking are intended to remind us of the beatitudes.

The nine ladies dancing honor the fruits of the Holy Spirit; Love, Joy, Peace, Patience, Kindness, Goodness, Faithfulness, Gentleness and Humility.

The ten lords-a-leaping reflect upon the 10 Commandments.

The eleven pipers-piping are the 11 faithful disciples of Jesus.

The twelve drummers drumming symbolizes the twelve tenants of the Apostles' Greed.

May the reason for this season fill your heart today and every day with the peace of the Lord.

Author's closing:

This reflection series would not exist if not for the encouragement of my family and friends.

In particular, I must thank my priest and good friend Rev. Canon Jim Shoucair for again providing appropriate scripture to enhance my humble reflections.

Further, I must again thank Amazon for first allowing me to publish this series as an e-book and today make it available in print.

For those who found comfort in this work, you may wish to explore my Lenten Reflections series titled, "Forty Shades of Love."

My Author's page can be found at the following url,

www.voicesof.us

Peace be with you my friends.

Semper Fi

23930619R00030

Printed in Great Britain
by Amazon